Just Us Women

Just Us Women

by Jeannette Caines

illustrated by Pat Cummings

HarperTrophy

A Division of HarperCollins Publishers

Library of Congress Cataloging in Publication Data
Caines, Jeannette Franklin.
    Just us women.

    Summary: A young girl and her favorite aunt share the
excitement of planning a very special car trip for just
the two of them.
    [1. Travel—Fiction. 2. Aunts—Fiction] I. Cummings,
Pat, ill.   II. Title.
PZ7.C12Ju   1982   [E]   81-48655
ISBN 0-06-020941-0   AACR2
ISBN 0-06-020942-0 (lib. bdg.)
ISBN 0-06-443056-1 (pbk.)
First HarperTrophy edition, 1984.

For Martha Ann Bullock Rodgers,
my very own Aunt Martha

—J.F.C.

For Christine and Arthur

—P.C.

Saturday morning is jump-off time.
Aunt Martha and I are going to drive
all the way to North Carolina
in her new car.
Aunt Martha says,
"No boys and no men,
just us women."

We made our list last week
and double-checked it every night.
Aunt Martha forgets things,
so I'm her reminder.

She picked up two road maps just in case.

Last year she forgot the maps and our lunch on the kitchen table.

I saved two shoe boxes to pack our lunch in.
One for fried chicken and bread
and one for cake and napkins.
We're going to wrap our food in waxed paper
like Aunt Martha did when she was little.

We'll stop at all the roadside markets

and buy all the junk we like.

And there won't be anybody saying,
"We can't stop,
we got to make it there before suppertime,"
or
"Oh no! We're not stopping again!"

If it rains we'll get out of the car and walk.
We'll say we walked in the rain

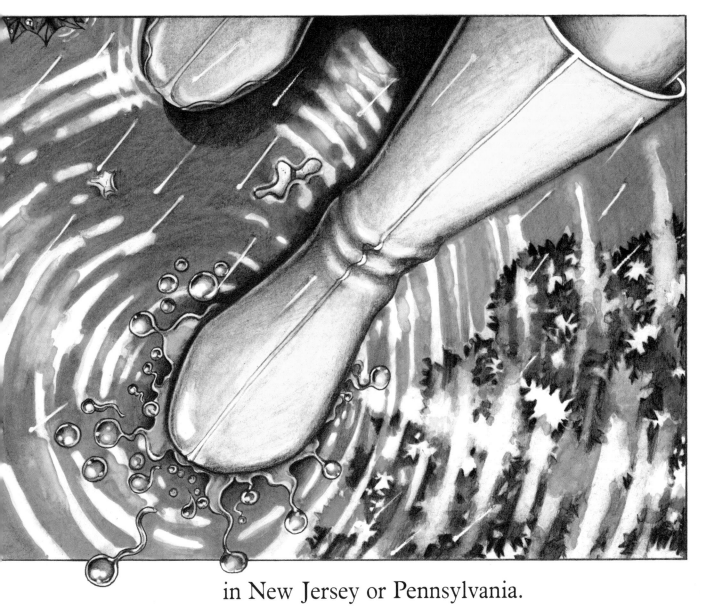

in New Jersey or Pennsylvania.
Last year we walked in Delaware and Maryland.

We'll mosey down the back roads
and talk to the farmers and buy their fruits.
And if the peaches are ripe we might get a bushel
and eat peaches from Virginia to North Carolina.

We'll stop and take pictures
in front of all the famous statues,

and when our chicken runs out,

we'll stop at a fancy restaurant.

Aunt Martha says
when it's warm and wet
the mushrooms are just right,
but we have to be careful
not to pick the poisonous ones.
We'll eat a mushroom omelette for dinner,
with coffee and tea.

We'll turn the day around and have our breakfast at night.

When we arrive, they'll all be waiting at the front door, saying,

"What took you so long?"

We'll just tell them
we had a lot of girl talk to do
between the two of us.
No boys and no men—
just us women.